CONTINENTS

Antarctica

Michael and Jane Pelusey

MACMILLAN
LIBRARY

First published in 2004 by
MACMILLAN EDUCATION AUSTRALIA PTY LTD
627 Chapel Street, South Yarra 3141
Associated companies and representatives throughout the world.

National Library of Australia
Cataloguing-in-Publication data

Pelusey, Michael.
    Antarctica.
    Includes index.
    For primary school students.
    ISBN 0 7329 9174 9.

    1. Antarctica – Juvenile literature. I. Pelusey, Jane. II.
    Title. (Series: Pelusey, Michael. Continents).
919.8

Edited by Angelique Campbell-Muir
Text design by Karen Young
Cover design by Karen Young
Illustrations by Nina Sanadze
Maps by Laurie Whiddon, Map Illustrations

Printed in China

Acknowledgements
The authors and the publisher are grateful to the following for permission to reproduce
copyright material:

Cover photographs: Penguins, courtesy of June Horner. Harp seal pup, courtesy of Corbis
Digital Stock.

All photographs © June Horner except Pelusey Photography, p. 6.

While every care has been taken to trace and acknowledge copyright, the publisher tenders
their apologies for any accidental infringement where copyright has proved untraceable.
Where the attempt has been unsuccessful, the publisher welcomes information that would
redress the situation.

Please note
At the time of printing, the Internet addresses appearing in this book were correct.
Owing to the dynamic nature of the Internet, however, we cannot guarantee that all
these addresses will remain correct.

Contents

Glossary words

When a word is printed in **bold**, you can look up its meaning in the Glossary on page 31.

Antarctica is a continent

Antarctica is the third smallest continent in the world. Look at a world map or globe and you can see the world is made up of water and land. The big areas of land are called continents. There are seven continents:

- Africa
- Antarctica
- Asia
- Australia
- Europe
- North America
- South America.

Borders

The borders of continents follow natural physical features such as coastlines and mountain ranges. Antarctica is a very large island surrounded by water. Its borders are all coastlines. The Southern Ocean surrounds the whole continent. Closer to the coast of Antarctica, the Southern Ocean is sometimes called the Antarctic Ocean.

 World map showing the seven modern-day continents

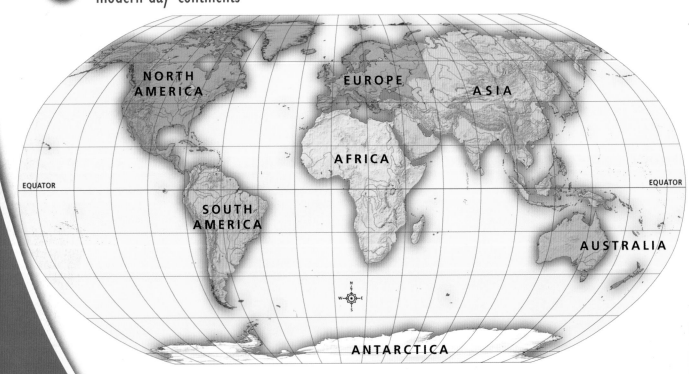

The world is a jigsaw

The Earth's crust is made up of huge plates, called **tectonic plates**, which fit together like a jigsaw puzzle. These plates are constantly moving, up and down and sideways, up to 10 centimetres (4 inches) a year. Over long periods of time, the plates change in size and shape as their edges push against each other.

Around 250 million years ago, there was one massive supercontinent called Pangaea. Around 200 million years ago it began splitting and formed two continents. Laurasia was the northern continent and Gondwana was the southern continent. By about 65 million years ago, Laurasia and Gondwana had separated into smaller landmasses that look much like the continents we know today. Laurasia split to form Europe, Asia and North America. Gondwana split to form South America, Africa, Australia and Antarctica.

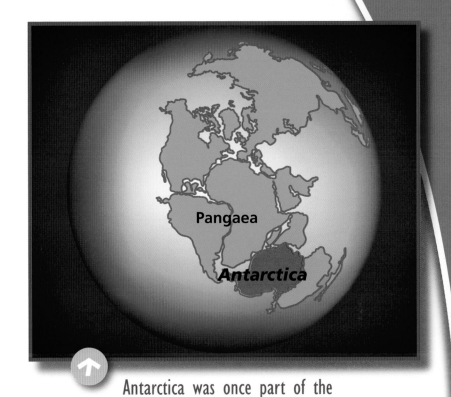

Antarctica was once part of the supercontinent Pangaea.

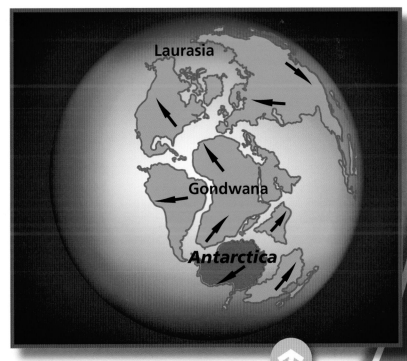

The Antarctic continent formed when Gondwana split into smaller landmasses.

Early Antarctica

When the continents were one, the landmass was much further north than it is today. The weather was warmer and wetter. There was light and sunshine every day. The continent was covered in plant life and animals. Scientists have found **fossils** of plants, animals and even dinosaurs in Antarctica similar to those on other Gondwana continents.

When Gondwana split and Antarctica was formed, the land moved south. As it reached colder regions, the plants could not survive as the land froze. In the middle of Antarctica, the sun does not set at all during summer, and it does not rise at all during winter. Plants cannot survive without light, so there are no plants in the middle of Antarctica.

Plants like this fern used to cover Antarctica when it was part of Gondwana.

Large glaciers move slowly towards the ocean.

Antarctic Ice Age

About 150 million years ago the Earth started cooling down and temperatures dropped around the world. Over millions of years the Earth's temperature dropped by about 10°C (18°F). Scientists believe the movements of the landmasses caused the change in the temperature that formed the **Ice Age**. During that period Antarctica became so cold that lakes and rivers froze. These frozen rivers of ice are called glaciers. They moved very slowly towards the coast of Antarctica carving out rock as they went. About three million years ago the glaciers reached the sea. Once these glaciers came into contact with the warmer water they started breaking up, forming huge blocks of ice. These icebergs spread around the whole continent surrounding it in ice and helping to keep the land cold.

Antarctica today

↑ Ice surrounding the mainland of Antarctica

Antarctica is about 14 million square kilometres (5.3 million square miles) in size. It is divided into two regions. The main landmass is called Greater Antarctica. The smaller part that looks like a tail is called Lesser Antarctica. Most continents are made up of one or more countries. Antarctica has no countries within its border.

The size of Antarctica changes from season to season. The pieces of ice that surround Antarctica are called ice shelves. In summer the warmer temperatures melt the ice making the ice shelf smaller. As the ice melts, huge icebergs break off and float out to sea. These icebergs eventually melt as they float into warmer water. In winter, as temperatures drop, the ice shelf increases in size. The difference in Antarctica's size from winter to summer can be as much as 1.5 million square kilometres.

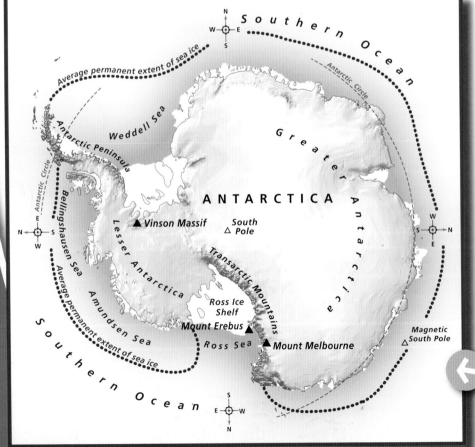

← The physical features of the Antarctic continent

The South Pole

There is more than one South Pole in Antarctica. There is the Geographic South Pole and the Magnetic South Pole.

Geographic South Pole

The Earth **rotates** around an imaginary line called an axis. The north and south of the axis are known as the North Pole and the South Pole. The Geographic South Pole is in the heart of Antarctica and is the point where everything else is north.

Magnetic South Pole

The Earth has a magnetic field. The north and south have opposite magnetic readings. A compass can find which direction is north or south. The South Pole from a compass is called the Magnetic South Pole. The Magnetic South Pole is always moving and ship captains adjust their map calculations every year so they know where they are.

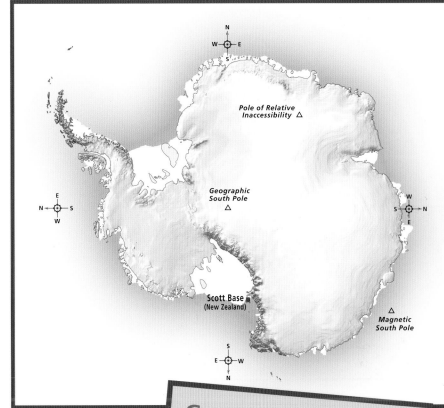

Centre of Antarctica

The centre of Antarctica is measured from the coastlines to the centre. It is called the Pole of Relative Inaccessibility.

New Zealand's Scott Base is 1353 kilometres (840 miles) from the Geographic South Pole.

SCOTT AA BASE

KILOMETERS TO	
SOUTH POLE 1353	CHRISTCHURCH 3832
WELLINGTON 4080	CANBERRA 4807
SANTIAGO 7079	BUENOS AIRES 760
CAPE TOWN 7408	TOKYO 12760
WASHINGTON 14828	PARIS 16708
MOSCOW 16899	BRUSSELS 16930
LONDON 17039	OSLO 17839

The land

Rock and ice form the Antarctic landscape. The rock is covered in ice and snow all year round. Only two per cent of the land is free of ice.

Mountains

Antarctica is a high continent. On average, it is 2300 metres above sea level. The highest peak on Antarctica is Vinson Massif in the Ellsworth Mountains. It is 4897 metres (16 067 feet) high. Antarctica is divided into two by the 4000-kilometre- (2500-mile-) long Transantarctic Mountain Range. These mountains separate two huge areas of ice called the East and West ice caps.

Volcanoes

Some mountains in Antarctica are active volcanoes. Mount Erebus is the highest at 3784 metres (12 414 feet). Mount Melbourne is smaller at 2733 metres (8966 feet). On the Antarctic Peninsula, hot volcanic water bubbles up from parts of the seabed and mixes with the cold sea water.

 Mount Melbourne is near the Italian base of Terra Nova Bay.

Glaciers

The glaciers of Antarctica stretch from the high regions towards the lower continent edge. There are thousands of glaciers on the Antarctic continent. Most are named after Antarctic explorers such as Taylor Glacier and Beardmore Glacier.

Valleys and lakes

Between the mountains are flat areas of land. The Dry Valleys are places that are almost free of ice and snow. There are two lakes in the Dry Valleys. Don Juan Pond never freezes completely because of salt and minerals in the water. Lake Vanda is always frozen on the top. Under the ice is a layer of cold fresh water and beneath that is a layer of warm water. The water is warm enough for **algae** and bacteria to survive.

Mars vehicles
The Dry Valleys are so barren they are used to test the unmanned vehicles that are sent to explore the planet Mars.

 Taylor Glacier flows into the Dry Valley.

11

The ice

When the top layer of water becomes cold enough it turns into crystals. As more crystals form, they join together to form young ice. Blocks of young ice hit each other and freeze together into a solid sheet. As the ocean underneath moves in waves the young ice breaks into circles called pancake ice. When ice sheets meet the frozen land they freeze solid forming fast ice. In summer, fast ice breaks off into pieces. These pieces move around the sea in groups called pack ice.

Icebergs

Icebergs are mountains of ice. Two-thirds of an iceberg is underwater. Large chunks of heavy ice shelf break away. They are often square so they are called **tabular** icebergs. Some tabular icebergs are bigger than small countries. Ocean currents can move them up to 65 kilometres (35 miles) in one day.

A tabular iceberg

A ship pushes its way through pack ice.

Most of the world's fresh water is frozen in the form of ice in Antarctica.

The world's water

The ice covering Antarctica can be up to 4000 metres (13 200 feet) thick. Nearly 90 per cent of the world's ice is found in Antarctica. Over 70 per cent of all fresh water in the world is in the form of ice in Antarctica.

Some scientists believe that air pollution is causing the Earth to get warmer. This is known as **global warming**. If the ice in Antarctica were to melt due to global warming, the seas would rise all around the world. Low-lying islands and coastal areas would become flooded, destroying cities and villages all around the world.

Towing icebergs

Some people have come up with an idea that ships could tow giant icebergs full of fresh water to dry places such as Australia. But there is a problem with this idea. What happens when an iceberg enters warmer water?

The ocean

The Southern Ocean surrounding Antarctica is made up of the southern parts of the Pacific, Atlantic and Indian oceans. Areas of ocean close to the Antarctic coast are called seas. They are mainly named after Antarctic explorers:

- Amundsen Sea
- Bellingshausen Sea
- Ross Sea
- Weddell Sea.

For many months every year the Southern Ocean is lashed by very strong winds that produce huge waves. The roughest weather in the Southern Ocean occurs outside the Antarctic region near 50 degrees **latitude**. Seas near the Antarctic coast tend to be calmer than out in the open ocean. This is because pack ice breaks up the waves.

Deep water

The water around Antarctica is very deep. Some areas of ocean are over 3000 metres (9900 feet) deep. Little is known about marine life in this deep water as scientists have difficulty getting there.

Floating ice makes the ocean calmer near the Antarctic coast.

Warm and cold water

Closer to Antarctica, there is a region where cold water from the icy continent meets the warmer Southern Ocean. The colder water is heavier and sinks below the warmer water. This reaction causes a sea mist to form. It is called the Antarctic Convergence. The area of ocean where this happens varies from season to season and from year to year. South of the Convergence the Southern Ocean is called the Antarctic Ocean.

Sea mist on the Antarctic Convergence occurs when the cold water from Antarctica meets the warmer water of the Southern Ocean.

Sea water freezing point

Fresh water freezes at 0°C (32°F). Sea water is salty and the temperature must be colder to make the sea water freeze. Sea water freezes at about −1.8°C (28.8°F). The saltier the water the colder it has to be to freeze.

The climate

The whole of Antarctica has an arctic climate. It is the coldest, windiest and driest continent in the world. In winter, the middle of Antarctica does not see sunlight for many months while in summer it is light all day and night.

Cold

The temperatures in Antarctica in the Southern Hemisphere are colder than temperatures in the Arctic in the Northern Hemisphere. The warmest summer month in Antarctica is February, when the temperatures range from −15°C to −45°C (−5°F to −49°F). In winter the temperature often drops to −70°C (−94°F). August is the coldest month.

People need to wear warm clothing to protect against the Antarctic cold.

Coldest temperature

In 1983 the world's lowest temperature ever recorded was at the Russia Antarctic Station of Vostok. It dropped to −89.6°C (−129.3°F). At that temperature a spilt glass of water freezes to ice before it hits the ground.

The whole continent of Antarctica has an arctic climate.

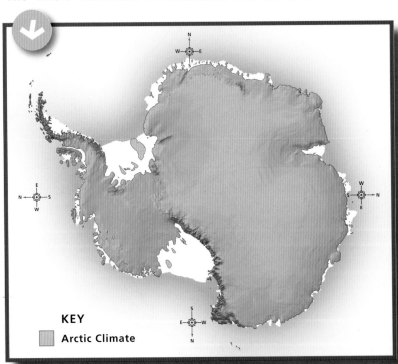

KEY

Arctic Climate

The interior of Antarctica has almost continuous daylight hours during summer. This photograph was taken at midnight during February in Antarctica.

Wind

Circulating around the Southern Ocean are winds blowing from the west called prevailing winds. In the colder higher parts, winds blow down mountain slopes with incredible force. They are called katabatic winds. Records show that Antarctica is the windiest place on Earth. At Cape Denison, the average wind speed is 72 kilometres (45 miles) per hour. Wind gusts there have reached over 240 kilometres (150 miles) per hour.

Dry

Although Antarctica is covered in ice and snow, it is the driest continent in the world. The large amount ice and snow has built up over millions of years. Antarctica gets less than 50 millimetres (2 inches) of rain a year.

 An approaching storm

The air is so dry in Antarctica that it can take more than 400 years for a dead animal to rot.

Plants and animals

The plants and animals that live in Antarctica have learned to survive in the extreme cold weather.

Plants

Small parts of Antarctica and surrounding islands are free from ice so some plants can grow. Most plants in Antarctica are tiny mosses and lichens. They are tough and can survive when frozen during winter then come back to life in summer.

Lichen and grasses grow in parts of Antarctica and on nearby islands.

Sea life

The waters around Antarctica are rich in krill, a tiny shrimp-like creature. Fish and whales roam these waters feeding on krill. Seals, penguins and albatrosses eat the fish. Leopard seals, that swim very fast and have sharp teeth, eat penguins. The killer whale or orca hunts in packs and eats seals.

Elephant seals

Blubber
Seals and whales all have a thick layer of fat called blubber that keeps them warm in cold water.

Birds

Antarctica has many birds that have adapted to the cold weather. Birds such as the wandering albatross glide above the rough seas searching for fish. Once a year they nest on rocky islands near Antarctica.

 The King Penguin carries its egg on its feet and tucks it under its fur to keep it warm and out of the mud.

Royal penguins coming to shore after fishing

Penguins

There are seven different kinds of penguins in Antarctica. During the **breeding season**, millions of penguins form big groups or colonies. Penguins swim fast to catch fish and escape leopard seals.

Female king and emperor penguins catch fish while the males look after the unborn chicks. He tucks the egg between his legs to keep it warm.

The largest penguin
The emperor penguin is the largest penguin at a metre (3 feet) tall. It is the only animal that spends the whole winter on the Antarctic mainland.

The people

Antarctica is the only continent with no permanent population. Visiting scientists and other workers spend up to a year at a time living in Antarctica to study the plants, animals and environment.

First sighting

Scientists in Europe believed there was a huge landmass in the Southern Hemisphere. Around 250 years ago Captain James Cook, an English explorer, discovered New Zealand and the east coast of Australia. From there he headed south but was stopped by icebergs in the Southern Ocean. Later, seafaring adventurers went further south finding islands inhabited by seals. They killed large numbers of seals, which they used to make oil from their blubber. The sealers moved on trying to find more islands inhabited by seals. This search took them further south into colder waters. It was not until 1820 that Antarctica was actually sighted.

 Old pots once used by seal hunters to boil dead seals to make oil.

Discovering Antarctica

- Thaddeus von Bellingshausen (Russia, 1820) sailed around Antarctica and was first to see the continent. He was followed by Edward Bransfield and Nathaniel Palmer.
- John Davis (United States of America, 1821) was the first man to set foot on Antarctica.
- James Weddell (England, 1823) reached the furthest south. He named Weddell Sea and the Weddell Seal.
- James Clark Ross (England, 1841) discovered and named the Ross Ice Shelf and Mount Erebus.
- Adrian de Gerlache (Belgium, 1897) led the first scientific expedition. When their ship became stuck in ice, they became the first people to spend winter in Antarctica.
- Carsten Borchgrevink (England, 1898) was the first person to spend winter on the Antarctic land and did the first sled trip on the Ross Ice Shelf.

Tourists visiting the remains of huts left by English explorer Carsten Borchgrevink.

Exploration ships

During the late 1700s and early 1800s European and American seal and whale hunters came close to the edge of Antarctica in large sailboats. Attempts were made to land on Antarctica itself, but the wooden boats of the time could not get through the pack ice.

Early explorers

In 1821, John Davis, from the United States of America became the first person to set foot on the continent of Antarctica. Other explorers quickly followed. Their aim was to be the first to reach the South Pole, which is a very difficult and dangerous journey. They built huts on the edge of the continent with supplies of food for the long stay. During winter and while waiting for the right weather conditions they did the first scientific studies of Antarctica.

Travelling to the South Pole was difficult because of the weather and ice. Explorers tried different forms of transport in the icy regions of the Antarctic. They brought sleds and teams of dogs and horses to pull them. These animal teams often failed, though, and the explorers had to pull the sleds themselves.

AFRICA

Captain Cook circumnavigates Antarctica, 1772–75
Amundsen's route to the South Pole, 1911
Scott's route to the South Pole, 1912
Mawson, David and Mackay's route to the Magnetic South Pole 1908–09
Mawson, Ninnis and Mertz's route to the Far East Sledging Party, 1912–13

SOUTH AMERICA

ANTARCTICA

Geographic South Pole

Magnetic South Pole (1908)

NEW ZEALAND

AUSTRALIA

Many explorers have visited Antarctica.

This is the hut where explorer Robert Scott and his team prepared for their expedition.

Race for the South Pole

- Robert Falcon Scott (England, 1901) failed to reach the South Pole with sled dogs.
- Otto von Nordenskjold (Sweden, 1901) failed to reach Antarctica and got stuck for two years. He did important scientific studies while waiting to be rescued.
- Ernest Shackleton (England, 1907) failed to reach the South Pole with horses.
- David Edgeworth (Australia, 1907) reached the Magnetic South Pole.
- Roald Amundsen (Norway, 1911) was the first man to reach the South Pole with sled dogs on 14 December.
- Robert Falcon Scott (England, 1912) reached the South Pole on 17 January (33 days after Amundsen). The whole team died on the return trip.
- Douglas Mawson (Australia, 1912) spent two years exploring and studying Antarctica.

Inside Scott's hut, supplies for the expedition are still on the shelves today preserved by the cold temperatures.

Early Antarctic explorers suffered great hardship trying to get to the South Pole. Fierce storms and freezing temperatures made exploration difficult. Some explorers froze to death, suffered snow blindness or **frostbite**.

Crossing Antarctica

Crossing Antarctica proved to be a bigger challenge for explorers than reaching the South Pole.

Ernest Shackleton

In 1914, explorer Ernest Shackleton planned to leave one ship at the Ross Ice Shelf and another ship on the other side of the continent. He and his team were going to walk 2900 kilometres (1800 miles) from one ship to the other. On landing at the Ross Ice shelf, his ship became stuck in ice and was crushed into splinters. They had to row lifeboats to an island 250 kilometres (155 miles) away. To save his crew, Shackleton rowed to a whaling station on the island of Georgia where he got help.

First Antarctic crossing

In 1958 Vivian Fuchs (Great Britain) and his partner Sir Edmund Hillary (New Zealand) became the first people to successfully cross the Antarctic continent.

The Ross Ice Shelf

Flying over Antarctica

Aircraft made it possible to further explore Antarctica. Exploration teams brought small planes by ship and made flights from their base camps. It was by plane that they were able to prove that the Antarctic Peninsula was joined to the rest of Antarctica. Flying in Antarctica is only possible in good weather.

Modern day explorers

Exploration continues in Antarctica today. In 1993, American Ann Bancroft led the American Women's Expedition to the South Pole using skis. She later teamed with Norwegian polar explorer Liv Arnesen to sail and ski across Antarctica's landmass. The 2747-kilometre (1717-mile) journey took 94 days.

In 1997, Norwegian Boerge Ousland became the first person to cross Antarctica unsupported, using only a sled, skis and a sail.

 Today, Antarctic exploration is often done using helicopters.

Crossing Antarctica by air

- Hubert Wilkins (Australia, 1928) was the first man to fly over Antarctica from his base camp.
- Richard Evelyn Byrd (United States of America, 1929) was the first man to fly to the South Pole from his camp.
- Lincoln Ellsworth (United States of America, 1935) made the first flight across Antarctica.

Scientists

In 1950, scientist Dr Lloyd Berkner suggested having an event called the International Geophysical Year. His plan was for scientists from different countries to work together to study Antarctica. Fifty countries agreed to the plan and 12 countries set up scientific research stations in Antarctica. In 1959, 12 countries signed the Antarctic Treaty. All the signed countries agreed to use the continent for peaceful purposes and to protect its wildlife, plants and natural environment.

Today, more than 40 countries have signed the Antarctic treaty and there are many scientific bases in Antactica run by different countries. The people who work at these bases travel there in strongly built ships called icebreakers. They move slowly through pack ice, breaking it up as they go.

The American Antarctic base of McMurdo Station with Mount Erebus in the background

An icebreaker cutting through pack ice

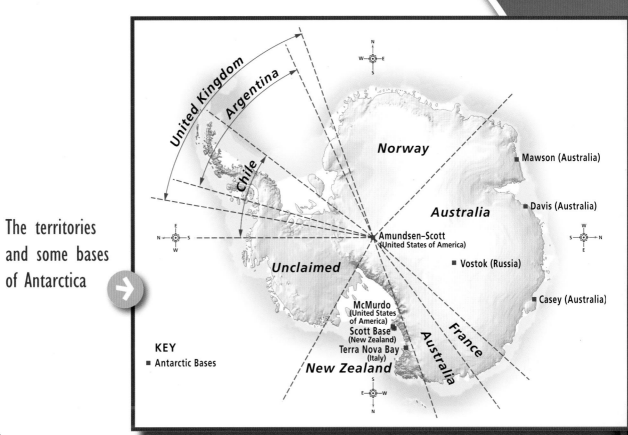

The territories and some bases of Antarctica

KEY
■ Antarctic Bases

Map labels: United Kingdom, Argentina, Chile, Norway, Mawson (Australia), Davis (Australia), Australia, Amundsen-Scott (United States of America), Unclaimed, Vostok (Russia), Casey (Australia), McMurdo (United States of America), Scott Base (New Zealand), Terra Nova Bay (Italy), France, Australia, New Zealand

Summer

The scientific bases in Antarctica are busiest during summer. Scientists study the weather, the environment, **geology**, wildlife, glaciers and the ocean. Doctors, chefs and engineers to look after the equipment also stay at the bases. People live in specially constructed buildings that are heated and have modern facilities. There are no shops in Antarctica, so all food and equipment has to be shipped in. When going outside, people must wear really warm clothing and be prepared for the weather, which can change very quickly.

Winter

Some scientists stay in Antarctica for the whole winter. They may go weeks without going outside because of freezing windy weather. They use telephones and email to communicate to the outside world.

Living quarters at McMurdo Station

Antarctica's future

Antarctica is an unspoilt environment. Unlike other continents, people have not built big cites, farmed the land or mined for minerals in Antarctica.

Challenges

Antarctica is facing a big new challenge. Tourists are now visiting Antarctica in big ships. Tourists are taken ashore in blow-up boats called zodiacs to see seals and penguins. Tourists, scientists and other visitors have to follow strict rules so as not to hurt the environment:

- Before leaving the ship, everyone's shoes are cleaned with disinfectant. People can bring diseases on their shoes that can kill penguins and seals.
- When people see wildlife such as penguins and seals, they must not go too close or touch them.
- All rubbish must be taken back on board the ship.

Tourists visit Antarctica to see animals such as King Penguins.

Goals

The main goal is to look after Antarctica. Scientists come to Antarctica because they can carry out experiments in an unpolluted environment. Many important discoveries have been made in Antarctica, such as the hole in the **ozone layer**. Because of this discovery, industries around the world now have to reduce air pollution, which is what caused the hole.

Countries that are members of the Antarctic Treaty are working to keep the continent clean and in its original form. In 2009, the Treaty will be 50 years old. It is important that the work done by the Treaty countries continues. In 1991 Treaty member countries placed a 50-year ban on the mining of minerals in Antarctica. Scientific research is important for the future of Antarctica, the world and even space.

 There is a fine balance between the impact of people and the Antarctic wildlife and environment.

Antarctica in review

Antarctica is the third smallest continent.

Area: 14 million square kilometres (5.3 million square miles)

Population: no people live permanently in Antarctica

Summer population: 4000

Winter population: 1000

Scientific stations: more than 40

First Antarctic Treaty: signed in 1959 by 12 countries

Current Antarctic Treaty: signed by more than 40 countries

Regions: Greater Antarctica and Lesser Antarctica

Highest point: Vinson Massif at 4897 metres (16 067 feet) high

Highest volcano: Mount Erebus at 3784 metres (12 414 feet) high

Climate zones: arctic

Species of birds south of the Antarctic Convergence: 43

Species of penguins: 17

Species of seals: six

Species of whales in Antarctic waters: 12

Websites

For more information on Antarctica go to:
http://www.antdiv.gov.au
http://www.glacier.rice.edu
http://www.coolantarctica.com
http://70south.com

Glossary

algae   plantlike organisms that live in wet conditions and do not have leaves, stems or roots

arctic   a climate of extremely cold temperatures

breeding season   when animals have their young at the same time every year

equator   an imaginary line around the middle of the Earth's surface

fossils   remains of animals and plants that have died

frostbite   when fingers and toes freeze, and are very painful as they defrost

geology   the study of the Earth's crust and its layers

global warming   the increase in the average temperature of the world

Ice Age   periods in the Earth's history when temperatures were much lower, and when water turned into ice

latitude   imaginary lines that go around the Earth surface. The equator is at 0° latitude. The South Pole is at 90° latitude.

Northern Hemisphere   the top half of the world above the equator

ozone layer   layer of the Earth's atmosphere that protects us from the sun's harmful rays

rotates   spins

Southern Hemisphere   the bottom half of the world below the equator

tabular   square and flat in shape, like a table

tectonic plates   large pieces of the Earth's crust that move slowly, causing earthquakes

tourists   people who visit other countries on holidays

Index

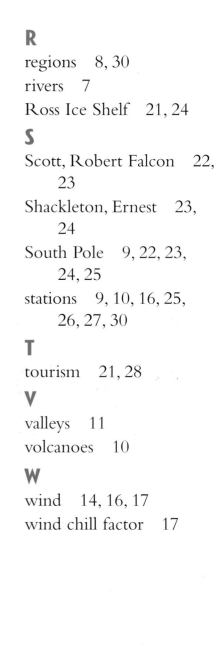